GUINNESS WORLD RECORDS

TOP ★ 10

Amazing Pet Records

Compiled by Ryan Herndon

For Guinness World Records:
Laura Barrett, Craig Glenday, Kim Lacey, Betty Halvagi, Stuart Claxton

SCHOLASTIC INC.
New York   Toronto   London   Auckland   Sydney
Mexico City   New Delhi   Hong Kong   Buenos Aires

The publisher would like to thank the following for their
kind permission to use their photographs in this book:

Cover, title page, 7: © 2005 Drew Gardner/Guinness World Records; 1: © Ryan McVay/
Photodisc/PictureQuest; 2: © Jose Luis Pelaez, Inc./CORBIS; 3: © Creatas/PictureQuest;
4, 5 (top): © Daily Mail/Solo Syndication; 5 (bottom): © Dragon/Rex USA; 6: © Royalty Free
Corbis/PictureQuest; 8: © Eliot Elisofon/Time & Life Pictures/Getty Images; 9: © G.K. and Vikki
Hart/Brand X Pictures/PictureQuest; 10: © Norbert Schaefer/CORBIS; 11: © MARK MOFFETT/
Minden pictures; 13: Courtesy of Guinness World Records; 14: Courtesy of Guinness World
Records; 15: © Tom Nebbia/CORBIS; 16 (top): © Arthur Tilley/i2i Images/PictureQuest;
16 (bottom): © Fredde Lieberman/Index Stock/PictureQuest; 17: © Ross Pictures/CORBIS;
18: © Gerard Vandystadt/Photo Researchers, Inc.; 19: © John Wright/REX USA; 20 (top):
© Photodisc via SODA; 20 (bottom): © BRYN COLTON/Rex USA; 21: © 2005 Guinness
World Records; 22: © Volker Steger/Photo Researchers, Inc.; 23: © Stephen Dalton/Photo
Researchers, Inc.; 24: © Frank Siteman/Index Stock/PictureQuest; 25: © Gary Allen/The News
and Observer/AP Wide World Photo; 26, 27: © Serpent Safari; 29: © Courtesy of Janice Wolf;
30: © Arthur Tilley/i2i Images/PictureQuest

Guinness World Records Limited has a very thorough accreditation system
for records verification. However, while every effort is made to ensure accuracy,
Guinness World Records Limited cannot be held responsible for any
errors contained in this work. Feedback from our readers on
any point of accuracy is always welcomed.

© 2005 Guinness World Records Limited, a HIT Entertainment plc company

Published by Scholastic Inc. SCHOLASTIC and associated logos are trademarks
and/or registered trademarks of Scholastic Inc.

ISBN 0-439-79188-X

Designed by Michelle Martinez
Photo Research by Els Rijper
Records from the Archives of Guinness World Records

18 17 16 15   40   11 12 13 14/0

Printed in the U.S.A.

First printing, September 2005

Visit Scholastic.com for information about our books and authors online!
Visit Guinness World Records at www.guinnessworldrecords.com

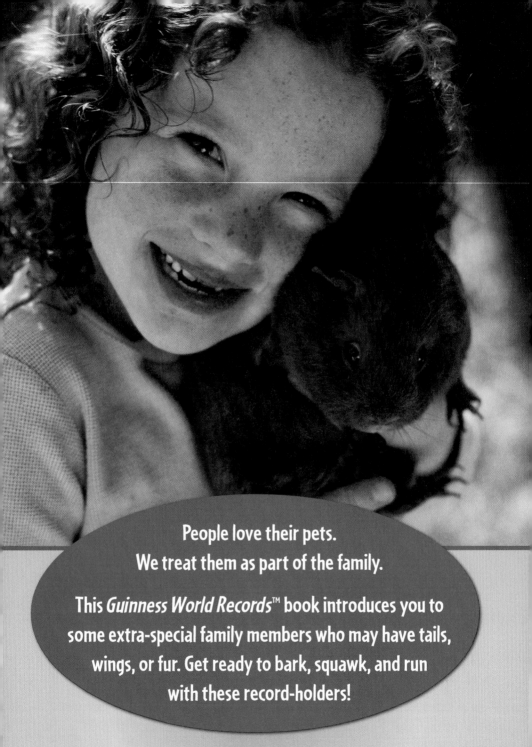

People love their pets.
We treat them as part of the family.

This *Guinness World Records*™ book introduces you to
some extra-special family members who may have tails,
wings, or fur. Get ready to bark, squawk, and run
with these record-holders!

MY FRIEND

Sometimes the world seems like a big, lonely place. A good friend promises to always be there for us. Friends come in many sizes and shapes. A pet proves that friends also come in many different species!

Choosing a pet is an important decision. Dogs and cats are the most popular pets. Thirty percent of the world's dogs and 40 percent of the world's cats live in the United States. But people also train guinea pigs, raise horses, talk with birds, and race snails.

Let's meet 10 Guinness World Record-holders who are also truly amazing pets! Which of these pets would you like to live with?

Wild animals should never be taken from the wild.

Most Extreme Sports Participated in by a Dog

Dogs are called "man's best friend." A Jack Russell terrier named Part-Ex stays with his best friend, a human named John-Paul Eatock . . . even when he's climbing cliffs!

One day, John-Paul saw Part-Ex jump from a cliff and dive into a waterfall on his own. The little dog was "cliff diving," an extreme sport John-Paul enjoyed, too.

When John-Paul went wind-surfing, Part-Ex jumped onto the board (left).

If John-Paul went kayaking, Part-Ex wanted the front seat (above). If John-Paul went rock climbing, Part-Ex leaped into his backpack for a free ride (below).

People wear safety equipment for extreme sports. Part-Ex wears a custom-made wet suit, a life preserver, a safety harness, and special boots to protect his paws.

Now when Part-Ex goes cliff diving, his best friend, John-Paul, always follows him!

John-Paul never forces Part-Ex to do a sport he doesn't want to do. Follow the same rule when teaching tricks to your pet.

Speak the command clearly, such as "sit," "stay," or "jump." Tell your pet, "Good job!" when it does the trick. Say "okay" to let your pet know that the trick is done. Reward it with a small treat (above).

Ask the **veterinarian,** or animal doctor, about teaching tricks and how to take good care of your pet.

Never make your pet do a trick it doesn't like doing.

Pets come in many sizes. The size and shape of an animal's body tells us the **breed,** or group, the animal belongs to.

Augie is a golden retriever. This breed is great at fetching or **retrieving** items. The Miller family taught Augie a trick that made him the record-holder for **Most Tennis Balls Held in Mouth**. On July 6, 2003, Augie retrieved and held five tennis balls in his mouth all by himself (below)!

Oldest Chelonian

People adopt or buy pets. Others receive pets as gifts. In the 1770s, British explorer Captain Cook gave the Tonga royal family a chelonian named Tui Malila (below).

Tortoises and turtles are **chelonians**. Tortoises live on land, while turtles live on land and in the sea. Tui Malila was a Madagascar radiated tortoise. The Tonga royal family took such good care of Tui Malila that 18 generations watched over him for 188 years!

Slow and Steady

If a tortoise raced a hare, who would win? Ask Chester, record-holder for Slowest-Traveled Pet.

In Aesop's story, the hare stopped hopping to take a nap. The tortoise's slow and steady pace won the race. In real life, hares hop about 30 miles per hour. Tortoises walk 3 miles per hour. Chester the tortoise escaped from his home in 1960. A neighbor found him in 1995. Chester took 35 years to walk just 2,250 yards! At that speed, it would take Chester 1 year and 310 days to walk the length of one football field.

Hop along and catch a rabbit record in this book!

Everyone is special
because each of us is
different—even our pets!
Guinness World Records
honors people
and animals
who are
the best at
what they do. Are
you a great runner
or jumper? Practice
your skills and, one day,
you may set a record. These
record-holders are the best at
being themselves in their
special size and shape.

Largest Frog

Andy Koffman loves frogs. On a trip to Africa in 1989, he made friends with an African goliath frog near Cameroon's Sanaga River. The frog measured 14.5 inches from snout to vent. Its powerful legs stretched out to 2 feet 10 inches. This frog tipped the scales at 8.07 pounds (right)!

Andy showed off his supersized frog on TV shows. When he tried to enter it in a county fair frog-jumping contest, other people got hopping mad! So Andy took his frog and went off in search of other huge frogs. And he found them!

Look out for more super jumpers!

Longest Cat

This Maine coon cat has a name almost longer than his body!

Meet Verismo's Leonetti Reserve Red (or Leo, to his friends). He measured 48 inches from nose to tail on March 10, 2002. That means Leo is as long as an 8-year-old kid is tall. His paws can fit into size-2 kids' shoes.

Not that Leo walks around in shoes. Instead, he hangs out with his owners, Frieda Ireland and Carroll Damron, who keep a careful eye on their big cat. He can even reach the kitchen counter!

WARNING!
Ask your vet about a pet's weight and diet. Guinness World Records does not accept records for fat, heavy, or skinny animals. DO NOT overfeed or starve your pets.

Leo is not a fat cat, just a long cat. He eats healthily and gets regular check-ups by his vet (right).

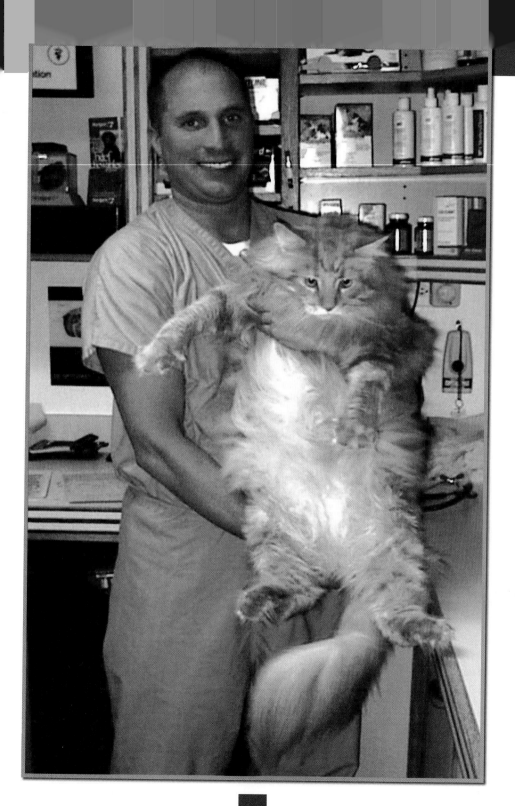

Tallest Living Horse

A system called **hands** measures a horse from its hoof to shoulder (or **withers**). One hand equals 4 inches.

Priefert Manufacturing, Inc., owns the tallest horse. Radar, a Belgian draft horse, holds the record at 19 hands 3.5 inches on July 27, 2004 (below).

Big animals have big appetites. Horses of this size eat about 50 pounds of hay and drink 30 gallons of water — every day!

TRAINING YOU

Could we ever talk with our pets like Dr. Dolittle did? The answer is Yes! Communication between owner and pet is important. Sometimes it can save lives. The key to understanding what animals are saying is to learn their behavior.

Behavior is how you act and react to things around you — how you move your face and body, how loud or soft your voice is. A dog may bark and wag his tail. After he sniffs your hand, maybe you can touch him. But a barking dog that shows his teeth, crouches low, and flattens his ears is warning you to stay away.

Spend time with your pets and watch their behavior. Does your dog stand near the door when she wants to go outside? Does your guinea pig hide if scared?

Pets do not know what behavior is good or bad. You must teach, or **train**, your pet. Sometimes a pet has trouble communicating with its new family. People called **trainers** are special teachers for animals (above). They teach animals and their owners new ways to communicate with each other. Ask your vet how you can train your pet.

Today, there's a show event for every type of pet. Judges inspect hundreds of pets and select the best ones in color, type, and athletic skill. Animals need special training to compete in these contests.

There are horse-jumping shows around the world (above). But other animals are also big leapers!

Highest Jump by a Rabbit

Bouncing this way is the rabbit record! Owned by Tine Hygom of Denmark, a rabbit named Mimrelunds Tösen (The Lassie of Quivering Grove) hopped an awesome 39.2 inches on June 28, 1997 (not shown).

Golden Flame used to be the record-holding rabbit. See her compete at another contest (below). Her owner used a special harness to guide her through the course.

And the Winner Is . . . !

You might think that some pets would never be able to win any awards. Would you ever think a guinea pig could win a high-jump contest? Well, it's true. Madde Herrman entered her pet guinea pig in a contest on March 16, 2003. Puckel Martin made the Highest Jump by a Guinea Pig at 7.8 inches (not shown)!

Even slow pets compete in speed races. Tortoises move at 3 miles per hour. An average garden snail slinks along at just 0.03 miles per hour . . . unless it's a racing snail. Hundreds of snails enter the annual World Snail Racing Championships every July in Congham, Norfolk, United Kingdom.

The snails start in the center of a 13-inch circular course and slink toward its outer edge (below). The Fastest Snail is Archie, trained by Carl Bramham, whose record-breaking sprint in 1995 lasted 2 minutes 20 seconds. Ready for another speedy slinker?

Fastest Ferret

About 15,000 pet ferrets are bought in the United States every year. Some run wire and cable for telephone and computer industries. Others enjoy the exciting sport of racing!

In Britain, ferrets are serious competitors in the annual North of England Ferret Racing Championships. On July 11, 1999, Jaqui Davis entered her pet ferret. Warhol became a champion with a 12.59-second dash through 32 feet 9 inches of plastic tubing (above)!

Most Intelligent Parrot

Having feathers doesn't mean you're bird-brained. Ask an African gray parrot (right). This breed speaks, or **mimics**, human speech.

Alex is the **Most Intelligent Parrot**. He knows words for more than 35 objects, 7 colors, and many-sided shapes. He can speak simple sentences!

Another African gray parrot, named Arthur, learns how to use a computer at the Massachusetts Institute of Technology (below).

Pets want to communicate with their families. There are times when knowing what your pet is telling you can save your life.

In December 1999, a gray parrot named Charlie became the record-holder for **Most Lives Saved by a Parrot**. Charlie squawked until Patricia Tunnicliffe and her family awoke and got out of their burning house. Sadly, it was too late to save Charlie. His family is forever grateful to him. There are hundreds of incredible stories about pets saving their families from danger. Learning your pet's behavior helps you to better understand each other!

MY HOME

Think about what makes your pet comfortable living in your home. Do you have a clean barn for your horse? Would a goldfish bowl fit on your desk? Your pet needs the right amount of space, proper care, and love to enjoy living with you.

Some snakes can be good pets — if you have the right environment, or **habitat**, for them to live in. Burmese pythons are popular pets (below). These snakes are large **constrictors**. They tighten, or **constrict,** their bodies around objects.

Always be careful when handling any animal, especially snakes.

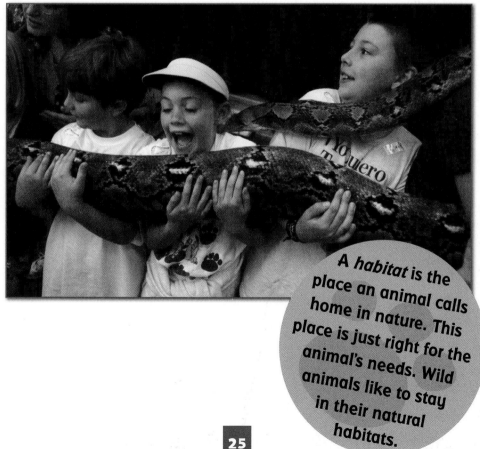

A *habitat* is the place an animal calls home in nature. This place is just right for the animal's needs. Wild animals like to stay in their natural habitats.

While Burmese pythons start out small, future owners must beware! Small baby pythons become big adults more than 18 feet long. They can weigh over 200 pounds, and eat seven chickens — for lunch! It may be best to visit these animals at the zoo.

Heaviest Living Snake

Lou Daddono owns Baby, a 21-year-old, 27-foot-long Burmese python. That's the width of one tennis court. She weighed 403 pounds on November 20, 1998. Baby lives in a home with lots of room and proper care at the Serpent Safari in Gurnee, Illinois (below).

Largest Horn Circumference for a Steer

Janice Wolf runs a group home for animals with special needs at the Rocky Ridge Refuge in Gassville, Arkansas. Her pet needs a lot of space for his special horns!

Lurch is a healthy and happy African Watusi steer. Many visitors, especially kids, are eager to touch his record-breaking horns. His horns are 7 feet long from tip to tip. The **circumference,** or thickness of each horn, got him into the record books. His horns measured 37.5 inches around on May 6, 2003 — about as big as an average adult man's waist. And his horns are still growing!

Born in Missouri, Lurch came to live with Janice when he was just five weeks old. She trained him to pose for the camera and give rides to his guests (right).

Janice takes her smaller pets to meet people of all ages at schools or nursing homes. Lurch is too big to go on these trips. His horns won't fit through any doors! He waits for people to stop by and visit him.

Guinness World Records keeps
track of the tallest, longest, bravest, and smartest.
It is our responsibility to make our pets feel the most loved.

Maybe the pet sleeping on your couch or jumping
around in your backyard is the next
record-breaker!